If you are a construction worker, this pocket guide is written for you. Small contractors should also find this information helpful. You are encouraged to go to the references in this document and to the OSHA website for more information.

This guidance document is not a standard or regulation, and it creates no new legal obligations. The guidance is advisory in nature, informational in content, and is intended to help construction workers and supervisors understand and reduce noise exposure on job sites. Employers are required to comply with safety and health standards as issued and enforced by either the Federal Occupational Safety and Health Administration (OSHA), or an OSHA-approved State Plan. In addition, Section 5(a)(1) of *The Occupational Safety and Health Act*, the General Duty Clause, requires employers to provide their workers with a workplace free from recognized hazards likely to cause death or serious physical harm. Employers can be cited for violating the General Duty Clause if there is such a recognized hazard and they do not take reasonable steps to prevent or abate the hazard. However, failure to implement these guidelines is not, in itself, a violation of the General Duty Clause. Citations can only be based on standards, regulations, and the General Duty Clause.

OSHA®
Occupational Safety and
Health Administration

Contents

OSHA
Occupational Safety and
Health Administration

Why is job site noise control important to me?

Exposure to high levels of noise can cause permanent hearing loss. Neither surgery nor a hearing aid can help correct this type of hearing loss. Construction sites have many noisy operations and can be a significant source of noise exposure.

Loud noise can also reduce work productivity and contribute to workplace accidents by making it difficult to hear warning signals. Hearing loss from loud noise limits your ability to hear high frequencies, understand speech, and reduces your ability to communicate, which can lead to social isolation. Hearing loss can affect your quality of life by interfering with your ability to enjoy socializing with friends, playing with your children or grandchildren, or participating in other activities.

Damage to your hearing **can be prevented**, but once permanent noise-induced hearing loss occurs, it **cannot be cured** or reversed. Hearing loss usually occurs gradually, so you may not realize it is happening until it is too late.

Noise can also **affect your body in other ways**. A recent study found that workers persistently exposed to excessive occupational noise may be two-to-three times more likely to suffer from serious heart disease than workers who were not exposed.[1]

---

[1]Gan, W. et al., Exposure to Occupational Noise and Cardiovascular Disease in the United States: NHANES 1999-2004, Occup Environ Med doi: 10.1136/oem.2010.055269.

Occupational Safety and Health Administration

You may have hearing loss if:
- You have a hard time hearing people in groups or meetings or if there is background noise.
- People sound as if they are mumbling.
- You have to ask people to repeat what they say.
- You have trouble understanding others on the telephone.
- You have ringing or noises in one or both ears.
- You have trouble hearing back-up alarms or the ringing of a cell phone.

How does hearing damage happen?

A one-time exposure to a sudden powerful noise, such as an explosion, may damage your hearing instantly. Prolonged exposures to loud noise can lead to a gradual, but permanent, loss of hearing.

Damage can occur within the ear at noise levels similar to that of running a lawn mower for eight hours. At first, this may cause a temporary loss of hearing that may last as long as 14-16 hours. With repeated exposure to high noise levels and periodic exposures to very high noise levels (e.g., with the use of nail guns), as is common at most construction job sites, your hearing may not fully recover. More often, the loss of hearing occurs slowly over time from exposure to moderate levels of noise. When that happens, the hearing loss becomes permanent. This is why workplace noise is sometimes referred to as a stealth long-term hazard – because it is a painless, gradual process.

OSHA®
Occupational Safety and Health Administration

Hearing loss occurs when cilia, tiny hair cells that line the inner ear, are damaged. At first, the damage happens to the cilia that receive the higher frequencies. Gradually, noise damages more of the ear and affects how speech is heard. If you hear muffled or distorted speech sounds, that may be an indication that a substantial hearing loss has already occurred.

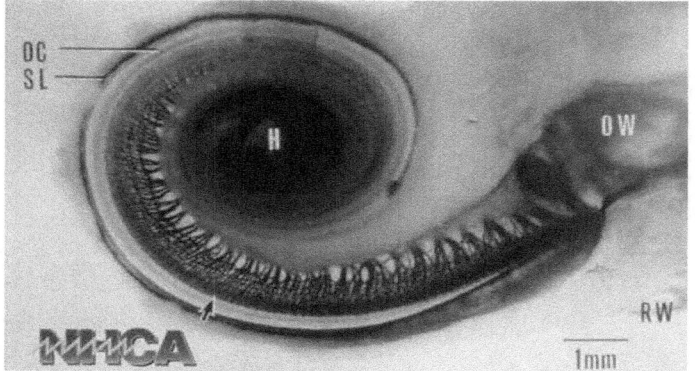

Healthy inner ear lined with cilia, tiny hair cells that help you hear.

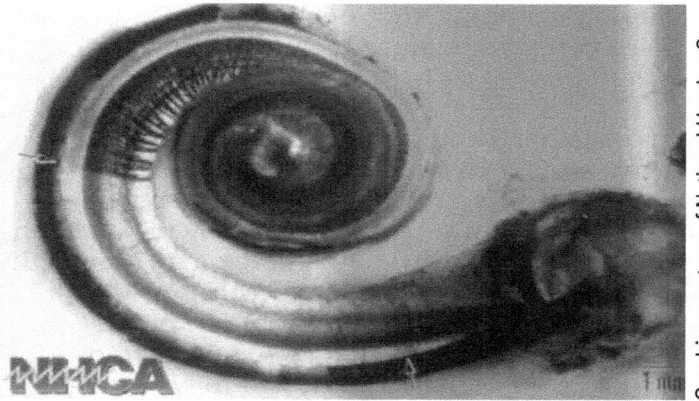

Inner ear showing damage to the cilia.

Graphics courtesy of National Hearing Conservation Association

In addition to hearing loss, you also may experience ringing in the ears. This is called *tinnitus*, and can occur even without other apparent hearing loss.

How do I know if my tools or job site are too noisy?

Sound intensity is measured in decibels. When decibels are adjusted for how the ear senses sound, the sound level intensity is measured as dBA. Decibels are measured on a logarithmic scale, which means that a small increase in the number of decibels results in a huge change in the amount of noise and the potential damage to a person's hearing. So, if the level increases by 3 dBA this doubles the amount of the noise and reduces the recommended amount of exposure time by half.

Sound Level Meter and Noise Dosimeter

Safety and health inspectors measure sound or noise levels using a device called a *sound level meter*. The microphone is positioned at the user's ear level. Equipment that is determined to be loud can be labeled with a hazardous noise sticker.

OSHA uses *noise dosimeters* to document the average noise exposure over your working day or of a particular task for part of your workday.

OSHA recommends that workplace noise levels be kept below 85 dBA as an 8-hour time-weighted average. As the noise level increases, it damages your hearing more quickly.

Sound level meter

Dosimeter

Images courtesy of Casella CEL Inc., Amherst, NH.

OSHA®
Occupational Safety and
Health Administration

Research indicates that your hearing can be damaged by regular 8-hour exposures to 85 dBA. When noise is as loud as 100 dBA (like a jackhammer or stud welder), it can take repeated exposures of as little as 1 hour per day to damage your hearing.

The National Institute for Occupational Safety and Health (NIOSH) has recommended that all worker exposures to noise should be controlled below a level equivalent to 85 dBA for eight hours to minimize occupational noise-induced hearing loss. NIOSH has found that significant noise-induced hearing loss occurs at the exposure levels equivalent to the OSHA PEL based on updated information obtained from literature reviews. NIOSH also recommends a 3 dBA exchange rate so that every increase by 3 dBA represents a doubling of the amount of the noise and halves the recommended amount of exposure time.

2-3 Foot Rule and Noise Indicator

When a sound level meter is not available, you should use the 2-to-3 foot rule: Stand about an arm's length away from your coworker: If you have to raise your voice to be heard 2-3 feet away, you should assume that the sound level is at or above 85 dBA.

A *personal noise indicator* is a warning device. It indicates if your immediate exposure is less than or greater than 85 dBA. It flashes green if the sound level is under 85 dBA and red when above 85 dBA.

Occupational Safety and Health Administration

Sound Level Chart

Equipment and daily activities at construction job sites can expose workers to high levels of noise. Sound levels on the chart below are listed in decibels (dBA) – the larger the number, the higher the volume or decibel level. How loud the noise is (volume), how long the noise lasts, and how close you are to the noise are all important in determining the hazard.

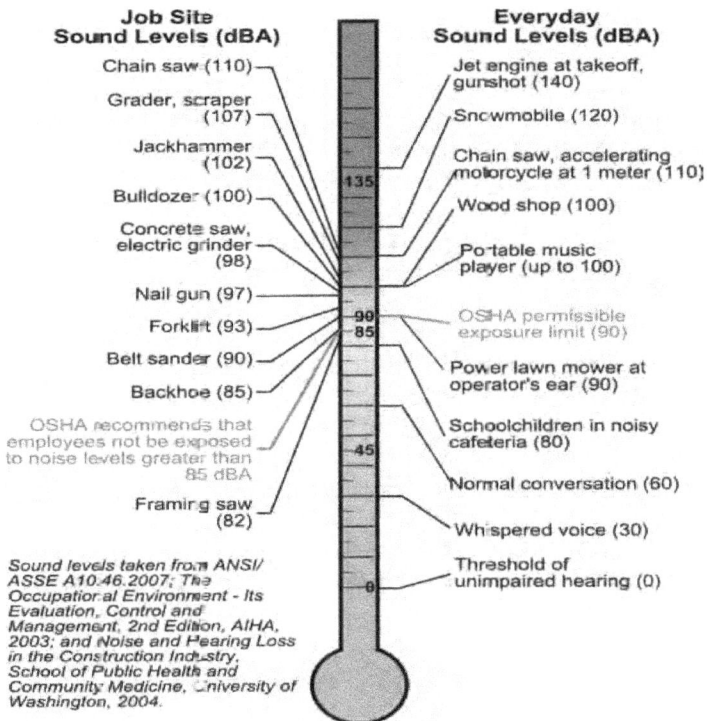

Job Site Sound Levels (dBA)

Chain saw (110)
Grader, scraper (107)
Jackhammer (102)
Bulldozer (100)
Concrete saw, electric grinder (98)
Nail gun (97)
Forklift (93)
Belt sander (90)
Backhoe (85)

OSHA recommends that employees not be exposed to noise levels greater than 85 dBA

Framing saw (82)

Sound levels taken from ANSI/ASSE A10.46.2007; The Occupational Environment - Its Evaluation, Control and Management, 2nd Edition, AIHA, 2003; and Noise and Hearing Loss in the Construction Industry, School of Public Health and Community Medicine, University of Washington, 2004.

Everyday Sound Levels (dBA)

Jet engine at takeoff, gunshot (140)
Snowmobile (120)
Chain saw, accelerating motorcycle at 1 meter (110)
Wood shop (100)
Portable music player (up to 100)
OSHA permissible exposure limit (90)
Power lawn mower at operator's ear (90)
Schoolchildren in noisy cafeteria (80)
Normal conversation (60)
Whispered voice (30)
Threshold of unimpaired hearing (0)

What can be done about job site noise levels?

Plan Ahead

One of the best ways to reduce exposure to hazardous noise on a work site is by planning for potential exposure before activities start. When jobs produce high noise levels, there are ways to reduce your exposure other than or in addition to hearing protectors.

For instance, your employer or supervisor can buy materials to build sound barriers or schedule noisy activities during hours when fewer people are working. Your employer can also rent or buy quieter equipment.

Your employer should hold daily or weekly safety meetings to discuss ways to limit high noise levels and other hazards. During safety meetings, the general contractor can ask sub-contractors to describe the planned tasks for the day or week where hazardous noise might be generated, as well as what equipment will be used; you can use these opportunities to talk about ways to limit exposure.

Even changes in the noise level that seem small (e.g., 3 dBA) are actually significant reductions in the noise.

> Here are some specific ways to limit exposure:
> - Plan to make or use prefabricated noise barriers.
> - Ask your employer to buy or rent quieter equipment/tools.
> - Limit the hours you work in hazardous noise areas.

Occupational Safety and Health Administration

- Identify equipment and work areas where signs can be posted to make other workers aware of high noise areas.
- Use hearing protection to supplement noise reduction.

Noise Control at the Job Site

The work site is where workers can have the most impact by working with employers to identify hazardous equipment, conduct hazard assessments, and apply the control process explained below. Employer support for providing supplies (acoustical insulation, extension cords, pre-fabricated noise barriers), hand tools, and sufficient set-up time are essential.

Noise Hazard Control Process

The easiest way to help lower noise levels at your work site is to remember a three-step noise hazard control process:

Reduce It: Reduce the noise by using the quietest equipment available. For example, choose a smaller, quieter generator.

Move It: Move the equipment farther away with the use of extension cords, additional welding leads, and air hoses (following current OSHA standards). Noise levels go down as we increase our distance from a noisy object. Move the generator farther away or face it in a direction that is away from where most people are working. If you are not required to be in a high noise area, move to a quieter area.

Block It: Block the noise by building temporary barriers of plywood or other on-site materials to keep the noise from reaching

Occupational Safety and Health Administration

workers. Place a five-sided, oversized wooden box over the generator. Add fire-resistant acoustical absorbing material (foam) inside the box. If the generator sits on soil or sand, that will help absorb some of the noise.

Building a plywood barrier

Maintain and Retrofit Equipment

Proper maintenance of equipment and tools can result in lower noise levels. Changing seals, lubricating parts, using sharp blades and bits, installing mufflers, and replacing faulty or worn equipment or parts can reduce the noise levels significantly on the job site.

Do you know of equipment on your job site that could benefit from regular maintenance to reduce noise levels? Your employer should ensure that there is a regular maintenance program and that everyone follows the maintenance schedule.

OSHA
Occupational Safety and
Health Administration

With some ingenuity, even older, noisier equipment can be modified by adding mufflers, new seals, or insulated panels. Employees can use noise reduction equipment accessories when made available by the employer. Employers can look for ways to reduce the sound intensity of tools in their current inventory.

Employers can reduce job site noise levels by following OSHA recommendations:
- Identify major noise sources and possible control solutions.
- Plan ahead and limit worker exposure as much as possible.
- Perform regular maintenance.

Reminder

OSHA currently allows your employer to rely on any combination of (1) hearing protective devices with a hearing conservation program, (2) engineering controls, and (3) administrative controls to effectively reduce worker exposures below 90 dBA.

OSHA also recommends that your employer provide – and that you use – hearing protective devices any time site exposures meet or exceed 85 dBA.

OSHA
Occupational Safety and
Health Administration

What can be done if engineering and administrative controls are not enough?

Proper Selection and Use of Hearing Protection

If other control strategies to reduce noise levels can't be used or fail to reduce noise levels below OSHA's permissible exposure limits (PELs), wear a hearing protective device (29 CFR 1926.52). There are many different types of hearing protection. Each type is designed for certain noise conditions. They include the types listed in the following table. But remember – unless you wear them properly and wear them all the time in high noise areas, the devices will not be effective.

Convenience and comfort are important for frequent use of hearing protective devices. Earmuffs and foam earplugs in most cases offer the most noise reduction. However, preformed plugs or canal caps may be more convenient where construction work generates moderate daily average noise levels. There is no one device that is the best type for all situations.

> **Your employer is responsible for selecting, fitting, and maintaining hearing protective devices and must provide them to you at no cost and train you in their use (29 CFR 1926.101).**

If you are not provided hearing protection for high noise work tasks, ask for it. If the employer refuses to provide hearing protectors, you can request an OSHA inspection.

Occupational Safety and Health Administration

Contractors and workers should consider the following when selecting and wearing protective gear: the noise level of the task, communication needs, convenience, comfort, hygiene, noise reduction of the hearing protective devices, and hearing ability.

Each type of hearing protection has manufacturer's directions for use and maintenance. Follow these directions and replace or fix the devices when they appear worn, dirty, or broken. Always wear hearing protection to protect yourself from high noise exposures, both on the work site and at home.

Neither portable music player headphones nor hearing aids are substitutes for hearing protective devices.

Regular Hearing Screenings

If you are routinely exposed to hazardous levels of noise, your employer should provide yearly hearing tests to monitor your hearing loss over time. If your employer does not provide these tests, you should have your hearing tested by an audiologist. The initial test (baseline) will be used as the reference test. Future tests should be compared to the baseline to see if you need to do more to protect your hearing.

These hearing tests can detect small shifts in hearing ability that have taken place since previous tests. When changes in hearing ability are detected, a retest is common to determine whether the change is permanent or temporary. Tests are relatively inexpensive and take about 20-30 minutes to conduct and get results.

OSHA
**Occupational Safety and
Health Administration**

Hearing Protective Devices

Type	Features	Concerns
Roll down foam	Fits many differently shaped ear canals. Provides good protection for most noisy environments. Convenient, disposable.	Must be inserted properly to get the highest possible protection. If the plug doesn't make a good seal, it won't protect your hearing.
Reusable earplugs	Many have flanges and handles. Come in different sizes. Come with cords, convenient to carry. Reusable. Washable.	Preformed so may not fit as wide a variety of ear canals as foam plugs. May require a different size for each ear. Must keep them clean.
Custom molded	Molded to user's ear. Always comfortable. Long-term wear. Best for difficult-to-fit ears.	Must be made by a licensed hearing protection provider.
Canal caps	On a band, can be worn under chin, over head, or behind neck. Can be put on and taken off quickly.	Not as comfortable as other devices. Not as much protection as other devices.
Earmuffs	Easy to use and wear. Fit most people. Easy to keep clean.	Can be hot and heavy. May be more difficult to get a good fit with glasses and/or may interfere with other protective gear.
New Types **Flat** **Attenuated** **Communication**	Flat reduction of noise over all frequencies. Have a baffle to reduce impact noise. Radio Communication while still reducing noise.	Can be expensive. Must be custom fitted.

Photos: NIOSH; Howard Leight; Aearo Technologies, a 3M Company; Bilsom; WorkSafe BC; Northern Safety and Industrial.

Remember:
***The best hearing protective device is the one
you'll actually wear.***

When looking at your hearing test, levels greater than 25 dBA indicate impairment. Furthermore, losses in the higher frequencies (3000, 4000, 6000 hertz) are more significant and you should discuss them with your audiologist.

You also can do daily monitoring of your hearing with a simple self-test. This works best if you drive yourself to work. When you reach your job site and are turning off the car engine, turn the radio on so it is just barely loud enough to hear (talk radio stations work well for this exercise) and go on with your day. When you return at the end of the work shift, check to see if you can still hear the radio with the power on, but the engine off. If you can't hear the radio, think about what may have damaged your hearing and how you could better protect your hearing.

Remember the 3 steps to noise control:
Reduce it: Use the quietest equipment available.
Move it: Locate noisy equipment away from workers.
Block it: Erect temporary barriers to block noise from reaching workers.

YOU ONLY HAVE ONE SET OF EARS – PROTECT THEM

OSHA®
Occupational Safety and Health Administration

My job site is too noisy. What can I do?

First, if you feel comfortable, speak with your supervisor. If you are a union member, raise the issue with your union representative. You can also call or write OSHA.

How do I file a complaint with OSHA?

• Mail, e-mail, or fax the nearest OSHA office (visit www.osha.gov or call 1-800-321-OSHA (6742) for the address of the nearest OSHA office) and request an inspection.

• File a complaint by phone – call (800) 321-OSHA (6742); the teletypewriter (TTY) number is (877) 889-5627.

• File online from OSHA's home page: www.osha.gov/as/opa/worker/complain.html.

Most online and phone complaints may be resolved informally over the phone with your employer. **Written complaints that are signed by a worker or representative and filed with OSHA are more likely to result in an OSHA inspection.**

Complete the OSHA complaint form, then fax or mail it back. Include your name, address, and telephone number so that we can contact you. All complaints are kept confidential.

OSHA
Occupational Safety and
Health Administration

Am I protected if I call OSHA?

The Occupational Safety and Health Act (OSH Act) prohibits employers from discriminating against their employees for using their rights under the OSH Act. These rights include filing an OSHA complaint, participating in an inspection or talking to the inspector or raising a safety and health issue with the employer.

If you believe that your employer has discriminated against you because you exercised your safety and health rights, contact your local OSHA office right away. Under the OSH Act, you only have **30 days** to report discrimination.

Call 1-800-321-OSHA (6742) and ask to be connected to your local office.

Discrimination can include:
• Firing or laying off
• Denying benefits
• Blacklisting
• Intimidation
• Denying overtime or promotion
• Reducing pay or hours
• Disciplining

OSHA®
**Occupational Safety and
Health Administration**

Additional OSHA Assistance

Compliance Assistance Specialists

OSHA has compliance assistance specialists throughout the nation who can provide information to employers and workers about OSHA standards, short educational programs on specific hazards or OSHA rights and responsibilities, and information on additional compliance assistance resources. Contact your local OSHA office for more information.

OSHA Consultation Service for Small Employers

The OSHA Consultation Service provides **free assistance** to small employers to help them identify and correct hazards, and to improve their injury and illness prevention program. Most of these services are delivered on site by state government agencies or universities using well-trained professional staff.

Consultation services are available to private sector employers. Priority is given to small employers with the most hazardous operations or in the most high-hazard industries. These programs are largely funded by OSHA and are delivered at no cost to employers who request help. Consultation services are separate from enforcement activities. To request such services, an employer can phone or write to the OSHA Consultation Program. See the Small Business section of OSHA's website for contact information for the consultation offices in every state.

- **Safety and Health Achievement Recognition Program**

Under the consultation program, certain exemplary employers may request participation in OSHA's Safety and Health Achievement Recognition Program (SHARP). Eligibility for participation includes, but is not limited to, receiving a full-service, comprehensive consultation visit,

correcting all identified hazards, and developing an effective injury and illness prevention program.

OSHA Educational Materials
OSHA has many types of educational materials available in print or online, including:
- **Brochures/booklets** cover a wide variety of job hazards and other topics;
- **Fact Sheets** and **QuickFacts** contain basic background information on safety and health hazards;
- **Guidance documents** provide detailed examinations of specific safety and health issues;
- **Online Safety and Health Topics Pages**;
- **Posters**;
- **QuickCards™** are small, laminated cards that provide brief workers' rights and safety and health information; and
- *QuickTakes* is OSHA's free, twice-monthly online newsletter. To sign up for QuickTakes visit OSHA's website at www.osha.gov and click on QuickTakes at the top of the page.

To view materials available online or for a listing of free publications, visit OSHA's website at www.osha.gov. You can also call 1-800-321-OSHA (6742) to order publications, to ask questions or to get more information.

NIOSH Health Hazard Evaluation: Getting Help on Health Hazards
The National Institute for Occupational Safety and Health (NIOSH) is a federal agency that conducts scientific and medical research on workers' safety and health. At no cost to employers or workers, NIOSH can help identify and correct potential health hazards in the workplace through its Health Hazard Evaluation (HHE) program.

Workers, union representatives and employers can request a NIOSH Health Hazard Evaluation.

OSHA®
Occupational Safety and
Health Administration

An HHE is often requested when there is a higher than expected rate of a disease or injury in a group of workers. These situations may be the result of an unknown cause, a new hazard, or a mixture of sources.

To request a NIOSH Health Hazard Evaluation, or find out more about the program:
• Call the NIOSH toll-free Information Service at 1-800-CDC-INFO (1-800-232-4636); or
• Go online at www.cdc.gov/niosh/hhe/Request.html.

OSHA
Occupational Safety and Health Administration

OSHA Regional Offices

Region I
Boston Regional Office
(CT*, ME, MA, NH, RI, VT*)
JFK Federal Building, Room E340
Boston, MA 02203
(617) 565-9860 (617) 565-9827 Fax

Region II
New York Regional Office
(NJ*, NY*, PR*, VI*)
201 Varick Street, Room 670
New York, NY 10014
(212) 337-2378 (212) 337-2371 Fax

Region III
Philadelphia Regional Office
(DE, DC, MD*, PA, VA*, WV)
The Curtis Center
170 S. Independence Mall West
Suite 740 West
Philadelphia, PA 19106-3309
(215) 861-4900 (215) 861-4904 Fax

Region IV
Atlanta Regional Office
(AL, FL, GA, KY*, MS, NC*, SC*, TN*)
61 Forsyth Street, SW, Room 6T50
Atlanta, GA 30303
(678) 237-0400 (678) 237-0447 Fax

Region V
Chicago Regional Office
(IL*, IN*, MI*, MN*, OH, WI)
230 South Dearborn Street
Room 3244
Chicago, IL 60604
(312) 353-2220 (312) 353-7774 Fax

Region VI
Dallas Regional Office
(AR, LA, NM*, OK, TX)
525 Griffin Street, Room 602
Dallas, TX 75202
(972) 850-4145 (972) 850-4149 Fax
(972) 850-4150 FSO Fax

**Occupational Safety and
Health Administration**

Region VII
Kansas City Regional Office
(IA*, KS, MO, NE)
Two Pershing Square Building
2300 Main Street, Suite 1010
Kansas City, MO 64108-2416
(816) 283-8745 (816) 283-0547 Fax

Region VIII
Denver Regional Office
(CO, MT, ND, SD, UT*, WY*)
1999 Broadway, Suite 1690
Denver, CO 80202
(720) 264-6550 (720) 264-6585 Fax

Region IX
San Francisco Regional Office
(AZ*, CA*, HI*, NV*, and American Samoa,
Guam and the Northern Mariana Islands)
90 7th Street, Suite 18100
San Francisco, CA 94103
(415) 625-2547 (415) 625-2534 Fax

Region X
Seattle Regional Office
(AK*, ID, OR*, WA*)
300 Fifth Avenue, Suite 1280
Seattle, WA 98104-2397
(206) 757-6700 (206) 757-6705 Fax

*These states and territories operate their own
OSHA-approved job safety and health plans and
cover state and local government employees as
well as private sector employees. The Connecticut,
Illinois, New Jersey, New York and Virgin Islands
programs cover public employees only. (Private
sector workers in these states are covered by Federal
OSHA). States with approved programs must have
standards that are identical to, or at least as effective
as, the Federal OSHA standards.

Note: To get contact information for OSHA area
offices, OSHA-approved state plans and OSHA
consultation projects, please visit us online at
www.osha.gov or call us at 1-800-321-OSHA (6742).

OSHA
Occupational Safety and
Health Administration

Appendix: More Information on Noise Protection

Here are some online references on noise control and hearing conservation:

***Construction Noise in British Columbia,* by the Workers' Compensation Board:**
http://hearingconservation.healthandsafety centre.org/pdfs/hearing/ ConstructionNoise.pdf

eLCOSH, the Electronic Library of Construction Occupational Safety and Health:
http://www.elcosh.org/en/browse/49/noise.html

***How Loud Is Too Loud?* A guide you can download with decibel levels:**
http://www.niccd.nih.gov/health/hearing/pages/ sound-ruler.aspx

Laborers' Health and Safety Fund of North America (LHSFNA):
http://www.lhsfna.org/noise

National Institute for Occupational Safety and Health (NIOSH) *Noise Meter:*
http://www.cdc.gov/niosh/topics/noise/ noisemeter.html

NIOSH *Power Tools* Database:
http://wwwn.cdc.gov/niosh-sound-vibration

OSHA's *Field Operations Manual:*
http://www.osha.gov/OshDoc/Directve_pdf/CPL_ 02-00-148.pdf

OSHA *Hearing Conservation for the Hearing-Impaired Worker:*
http://www.osha.gov/dts/shib/shib122705.html

OSHA *Noise and Hearing Conservation eTool:*
http://www.osha.gov/dts/osta/otm/noise/index.html

OSHA *Noise and Hearing Conservation Safety and Health Topics Page:*
http://www.osha.gov/SLTC/noisehearing conservation/index.html

Standards for States with OSHA-approved State Plans:
http://www.osha.gov/dcsp/osp/statestandards.html

The personal hearing protection devices chart on page 14 was adapted from *Toolbox Talks: Hearing Conservation in the Shipbuilding Industry,* **developed through the Alliance Program, an OSHA Cooperative Program:**
http://www.shipbuilders.org/Portals/Shipbuilders/ PP PDFs/Tool Box Talk series - hearing conservation in Shipbuilding - FINAL - 042409.pdf

What Causes Tinnitus?:
http://www.nidcd.nih.gov/health/hearing/tinnitus. htm#2

OSHA
Occupational Safety and Health Administration

(800) 321-OSHA (6742)

www.ingramcontent.com/pod-product-compliance
Lightning Source LLC
Chambersburg PA
CBHW051829170526
45167CB00005B/2215